Remembering
San Francisco
in the 50s, 60s, and 70s

Rebecca Schall

TURNER
PUBLISHING COMPANY

Ocean Beach is pictured on October 14, 1961. San Franciscans recognize that the fall is the nicest and warmest time of the year in the city and take full advantage of the Indian Summer days, knowing full well that each could be the last one before the rainy season begins.

Remembering
San Francisco
in the 50s, 60s, and 70s

Turner Publishing Company
4507 Charlotte Avenue • Suite 100
Nashville, Tennessee 37209
(615) 255-2665

Remembering San Francisco in the 50s, 60s, and 70s

www.turnerpublishing.com

Library of Congress Control Number: 2011943137

ISBN: 9781596527225

Printed in the United States of America

ISBN: 978-1-68336-882-3 (pbk)

Contents

This 1950s photograph, taken from the heights of Lupin and Laural above the intersection of Bush Street and Presidio Avenue, provides a panorama of San Francisco. Apartments at this intersection provide some of the best views in San Francisco today. In the foreground is a large streetcar yard of San Francisco Municipal Railway, and today the site houses half of San Francisco's electric trolley buses.

ACKNOWLEDGMENTS

For San Franciscans and San Francisco aficionados everywhere.

Thank you to my family—Fran Schall, Gerry Schall, Teddy Schall, Pedie Schall, and my grandma, Bess Berger, for your unequivocal benevolence, collaboration, support, and humor. Special thanks to Marc Levin; Christina Moretta, photo curator and librarian at the San Francisco History Center at the San Francisco Public Library; and Bradley D. Cook, curator of photographs at the University Archives and Record Center of Indiana University; and to all the beats, hippies, and counterculture revolutionaries that flourished during San Francisco's renaissance and contributed immeasurably to the national significance and cultural legacy of the city.

PREFACE

San Francisco is one of the world's great cities, known worldwide for its diversity, natural beauty, quality of life, culture, and cuisine. San Francisco, a beacon of the country, has always been an avant-garde, bohemian, extravagant, and intellectual city, which has historically drawn anyone slightly out of step with mainstream America and wanting to try out new styles of living. Much of what happens to the country usually starts in California, more often in San Francisco, the cultural, social, and political powerhouse of the state.

The city has come a long way since its humble beginnings as a rough-and-tumble frontier town and recovered tremendously from the ashes of the 1906 Earthquake and fires that nearly destroyed it. It took center stage during World War II as a major port of supplies and embarkation to the Pacific Theatre. San Francisco was the hub of activity for the major counterculture movements of the 1950s through the 1970s, becoming a center for the emergence of the Beat movement in the 1950s in San Francisco's North Beach, the hippie movement in the 1960s in the Haight-Ashbury District, and the continuing civil-rights and gay-rights movements in the Castro in the 1970s. Although San Francisco's Presidio acted as a vital military base and figured prominently in American wars from the late nineteenth through the mid-twentieth century, San Francisco became a fervently antiwar city by the 1950s, 1960s, and 1970s. The social ferment of the 1960s forever changed how young people felt about themselves, and they migrated to San Francisco by the tens of thousands out of a sense of adventure, idealism, and unlimited possibilities.

The music of the 1960s and 1970s, such as the Rolling Stones, Janis Joplin, the Doors, and the British invasion of the Beatles, invited resistance to the established order and alerted people to other ways of living. They rejected all that their parents' generation had valued. Groups were forged in this era of identity politics: gay rights, women's rights, Black Power, Red Power, and civil rights in general. This activism carried into the next decade, when women fought for equality and gays fought for acceptance and protection under the law in society.

When photography emerged in France in the nineteenth century, it allowed people to capture the modern world and document its history in unprecedented ways. The power of photographs is that they are less subjective than text in their treatment of the past. Although the photographer can make decisions regarding subject matter and how to capture and present it, photographs do not allow the same opportunity for incorporation of opinion and bias as text does. For this reason, photographs offer an original and untainted perspective that allow the viewer to observe, experience, and interpret for themselves. Thousands of historic photos of San Francisco reside in archives, and while those photographs are of great interest to many, they are not always easily accessible.

This book is the result of countless hours of reviewing thousands of photos in the San Francisco Public Library Archives, as well as extensive historical research. I greatly appreciate the generous assistance of my family and others listed in the acknowledgments of this work, without whom this book could not have been possible.

The goal in publishing this work is to provide a broader access to extraordinary photographs that will inspire, educate, and preserve with proper respect and reverence the story of San Francisco during these turbulent and formative decades. The photographs selected have been reproduced in their original black-and-white format to provide depth to the images. With the exception of touching up imperfections caused by the damage of time, no other alterations have been made.

This book is divided into three chapters, representing San Francisco in the 1950s, 1960s, and 1970s, respectively. In each section, *Remembering San Francisco in the 50s, 60s and 70s* attempts to capture various aspects of daily life in the city and provide a broad perspective of the historical significance of these divisive and decisive decades, illustrated by the selection of photographs, which feature important people, places, events, architecture, commerce, transportation, and scenes of everyday life. I encourage readers to reflect on this paramount time as they gain a new appreciation for the momentous history, unique character, and cultural and social influence of San Francisco in the latter half of the twentieth century.

—*Rebecca Schall*

Commuters cross from the Southern Pacific Depot at 3rd and Townsend to catch the new #30 Stockton trolley bus on January 20, 1951, its first day of service. This Muni bus line, today one of the busiest in San Francisco, replaced the F Stockton streetcar, one of many streetcar lines to be superseded by electric and diesel buses during the 1950s. Years later, the F Market historic streetcar line resumed use of the F name, although the two lines did not have any part of their route in common. The 1914 Southern Pacific Depot was replaced in 1975 by a new train station at 4th and Townsend, and the former location is currently the site of retail stores and a high-rise apartment complex.

The 1950s:

The San Francisco Renaissance, Post-War Prosperity, Nuclear Anxiety, and the Beat Generation

The University of Michigan band is playing at Seals Stadium on January 2, 1952. After a downtown parade, the 150-piece band, hailed at the time as the best in the nation, performed before 2,500 enthusiastic fans. Seals Stadium was built in 1931 at 16th and Bryant streets for the city's two minor-league baseball teams, the Seals and the San Francisco Missions. The Seals became the stadium's sole occupant in 1938 and played until the New York Giants moved to San Francisco in 1958. The Giants played in Seals Stadium for two seasons before moving to Candlestick Park in 1960. After Seals Stadium was demolished in 1959, the location was converted to a mall and then a car dealership. Currently, the site houses a shopping center. The memory of San Francisco's longtime minor-league baseball team lives on in Lou Seal, the official mascot of the San Francisco Giants, as well as the commemorative statue along the waterfront outside AT&T Park.

On March 17, 1951, 60,000 spectators cheer during the St. Patrick's Day Parade, which jammed up traffic along Market Street all the way to San Francisco's City Hall. One of many cultural celebrations in the city, the annual St. Patrick's Day Parade in San Francisco, which typically includes more than 5,000 participants from all over the country, is the largest one west of the Rocky Mountains and has always been popular because of the large Irish-American population in San Francisco. The Ferry Building can be seen along the waterfront at the end of Market Street in the background.

Maiden Lane is pictured here on March 30, 1951, during its Spring Festival. For many years, the Maiden Lane Merchants Association held an annual "Spring Comes to Maiden Lane" celebration. Maiden Lane, the two-block pedestrian street between Stockton and Kearny, has a sordid history, yet one would never know by looking at the posh high-end boutiques and outdoor cafes that line the street today. Known as Morton Street in the nineteenth century, this thoroughfare was saturated with more legal brothels than any other place in San Francisco and averaged one murder every week. Destroyed in the 1906 Earthquake, the street was renamed Maiden Lane in recognition of its unsavory past.

Louis Sutter, president of the Recreation Park Commission; singer Beatrice Kay; and San Francisco mayor Elmer E. Robinson are pictured on April 4, 1951, at the opening of a new nine-hole golf course off the main drive in Golden Gate Park. As the mayor took a swing, Louis Sutter acted as a caddy. The mayor missed the ball, and the singer yelled "fore" anyway. Today, the beginner-friendly Golden Gate Park Golf Course continues to be a favorite of locals.

During a gun salute in a memorial ceremony honoring merchant marines, an honor rifle squad of cadets from the California Maritime Academy in Vallejo is pictured on May 22, 1951. They are standing on the Golden Gate Bridge center span as a wreath is cast into the Pacific Ocean during World Trade Week.

Striking employees dressed in nightgowns are shown on the picket line at the Pacific Telephone and Telegraph Company's 25th and Mission streets telephone exchange on July 24, 1951. The ladies came to picket at 6:30 a.m. dressed in pajamas and wearing signs saying, "I can dream, can't I?" Written on the back of the photo was, "In case you're worried, they've got street clothes under the nightgowns." This office, along with the P.T.T. offices in Oakland and many other locales in Northern California, had been picketed for almost a week. Eight hundred workers, members of the C.I.O. Communications Workers of America, walked off their jobs at the Bush Street and Grant Avenue exchanges to protest what union officials charged as a lockout of plant employees who observed the picket lines.

Picketers on September 21, 1951, around the U.S. Post Office Building at 7th and Mission streets, protest the bail policy of assistant U.S. attorney Ernest A. Tolin for 12 westerners accused of being Communist Party leaders. The picketers were part of the California Emergency Defense Committee, but other marchers identified themselves as affiliates of the "Communist In-line Civil Rights Congress." During the Cold War, many feared that Communism would spread in America—fears confirmed with trials of Americans who had shared secrets with the Soviets. In 1947, Truman ordered four million government employees to take loyalty oaths and get checked out. The movie industry began to be targeted, with people's names appearing on unofficial lists of suspected Communists. Republican senator Joseph McCarthy crusaded against supposed Communists in the U.S. government, resulting in thousands of ruined lives, careers, and reputations. McCarthyism now refers to irrational charges against innocent citizens.

Dozens of youngsters play on the slides and swings at Children's Playground in Golden Gate Park on July 18, 1951, watched by their mothers. Opened as the nation's first public playground for children in 1887, the expansive grounds at one time featured such attractions as a bear pit and elephant rides, in addition to the slides, play structures, and carousel that have been longtime favorites. The playground was extensively renovated in 2007 and reopened as the Koret Children's Quarter.

On February 16, 1952, a ceremony is held in Golden Gate Park near a monument honoring Apperson Hearst to commemorate the 55th anniversary of the founding of the National Congress of Parents and Teachers by Phoebe Apperson Hearst and Alice McLellan Birney. Holding a wreath that was laid at Hearst Memorial Fountain is Mrs. E. M. Hood, President, S.F. District, Parents-Teachers. With her are Mrs. George M. Hearst (left), a past president who was a ceremony speaker, and Mrs. George W. Chambers, chairperson of the day.

Another early and very popular business at the Stonestown shopping center was Walgreens Drugstore. The interior of that Walgreens outlet is pictured here on November 21, 1952. Walgreens, which started in 1901 in Dixon, Ill., as a neighborhood pharmacy, has proliferated and is now one of America's largest drugstore chains, with one seemingly located every few blocks in San Francisco.

A customer waits for his order at the ice-cream counter at the Crystal Palace Market in the fifties. Opened in 1923 at 9th and Market, the market had numerous stalls where individual merchants sold fruits and vegetables, meats, cheese, drugs, jewelry, and tobacco and offered many consumer services.

A woman stands behind a counter at the Crystal Palace Market selling some sort of slimming concoction. One of the most popular of the independent merchants at Crystal Palace Market for many years, known as the Snake Man, used garter snakes to attract a large crowd around his stall, where he sold a special soap said to cure acne and other skin irritations.

Andre La Forgia stands behind a meat counter at the Crystal Palace Market. Another popular stall in the Crystal Palace Market was operated by the Anchor Brewing Company, which sold the locally brewed steam beer that is still popular today.

The new beach house at China Beach is dedicated in August 1954 by Supervisor James Leo Halley. The $140,000 beach house, very expensive for the time, contained a lobby, check room, first-aid station, shower rooms and lockers for men and women, lifeguard room, refreshment concession, and rooftop observation area. Although the beach house is run-down today, sunbathers still bask on the rooftop observation deck on warm days, and many people stroll along the beach to enjoy the spectacular views of the Golden Gate Bridge, Marin County, and the Pacific Ocean.

Nancy Menhennet and three friends are pictured standing atop a cliff at Land's End on April 25, 1955, watching the Coast Guard search for her missing brother and his friend. Each year, the U.S. Coast Guard is called upon to rescue people who have climbed out on the rocks near Land's End, China Beach, and Baker Beach and become stranded when the tide is in.

This 1952 photograph depicts the exterior of the Sutro Baths overlooking Ocean Beach. The beach, along the Pacific Ocean on the western shores of San Francisco, was developed in the late nineteenth century as a resort destination featuring the Cliff House and Sutro Baths. Trains took people from downtown through the undeveloped western end of the city, still known as the "Outside Lands." The Sutro Baths, once the world's largest indoor swimming pool, opened to the public on March 14, 1896. They consisted of seven pools and had a seating capacity of up to 8,000. The building was covered in 100,000 glass panes to allow for maximum sunlight to illuminate the building. Adolph Sutro (1830–1898), a Prussian immigrant, engineer, and former San Francisco mayor, built the baths. The Sutro Baths also housed a concert hall and museum with Sutro's personal collection of art, artifacts, and other curiosities.

Seal Rocks and the world-famous Cliff House are pictured here in the 1950s. The Cliff House, immortalized in postcards, is one of San Francisco's oldest and best-known tourist attractions and overlooked the former Sutro Baths. For years, it has been a restaurant that sits atop the cliffs north of Ocean Beach. The Cliff House has gone through five incarnations over its history, which dates back to the 1860s. In 1896, Adolph Sutro built the famous seven-story Victorian chateau Cliff House, nicknamed "The Gingerbread Palace." Although it survived the 1906 Earthquake, it burned to the ground on September 7, 1907. Within two years, Sutro's daughter built a new Cliff House in neoclassical style, which remains the Cliff House San Franciscans know today. Tourists can still dine at the historic Cliff House, look out over the ghostly ruins of the baths below, and see the famous Camera Obscura on the site.

Playland at the Beach was the world-famous ten-acre amusement park next to Ocean Beach by the Cliff House and Sutro Baths along the Great Highway between Cabrillo and Balboa streets. In the nineteenth century, the area, nicknamed Mooneysville-by-the-Sea was inhabited mostly by squatters. Over the first part of the twentieth century, independently owned and operated concessions, amusement rides, games stands, dance halls, and a variety of food stands and restaurants gradually sprung up at the beach. In 1926, George Whitney, known as "Barnum of the Golden Gate," became the general manager and officially named the park Playland at the Beach. This picture, taken on March 20, 1952 at the base of Sutro Heights, shows the Little Theatre, where a life-sized reproduction of Leonardo Da Vinci's masterpiece *The Last Supper* was on display; Musée Mechanique with its collection of antique, coin-operated music and arcade machines; the Rifle Range; and a concession where tasty Bull Pupps were sold.

A group of kids is pictured on August 9, 1955, leaning over at a Playland booth featuring a ring-throwing game. Three generations of San Franciscans enjoyed Playland's shooting gallery, Skee Ball, and numerous other midway games and dreamed of winning one of the stuffed animals or other prizes seen in the background in the picture.

A group of young boys, "knothole gang" members, peer through holes in a wooden fence at Kezar Stadium, some whittling larger holes for a better view of the championship heavyweight boxing match between Rocky Marciano and Don Cockell on May 17, 1955.

For millions of Americans, buying a home was the American dream. People wanted stability and a refuge from the troubles of their earlier lives, and activity was centered on the home and family. In this 1950s photograph looking west from Noe Street, the row houses lining 21st Street all look the same. Noe Valley is situated in central San Francisco, with the Castro Dsitrict to its north and the Mission District to its east. Named after Jose de Jesus Noe, the last Mexican mayor of Yerba Buena (now San Francisco), Noe Valley was developed in the late 1800s and early 1900s and contains some excellent examples of pre–1906 Earthquake Victorian and Edwardian homes. Considered upscale today, Noe Valley has the highest number of row houses in the city, built originally as efficient and inexpensive homes.

Chinatown is pictured here in the fifties, looking north on Grant Avenue from California Street. San Francisco is home to North America's oldest and largest Chinatown (ca. 1850s), bordered on the west by Nob Hill, on the east by the financial district, and on the north by North Beach. Tens of thousands of Chinese began to immigrate to San Francisco during the Gold Rush, seeking prosperity in the gold mines, and later working on building of the Transcontinental Railroad. Grant Street is Chinatown's main thoroughfare, named in honor of the 18th U.S. president, Ulysses S. Grant. After the start of the Gold Rush and the establishment of Chinatown, Dupont Street, as it was then known, became the district's most important street. It quickly earned a seamy reputation for the opium dens, brothels, and sing-sing girls on the street along the notorious Barbary Coast.

In the decade following World War II, some older homes in San Francisco that had fallen into disrepair were torn down and replaced by more-modern housing. Pictured here on January 25, 1953, is an old frame house at the southwest corner of Franklin and Jackson streets, roughly a year before it was razed. Mayor George Christopher and Justin Herman, head of the Redevelopment Agency, began a campaign to tear down "blighted" areas of the city, mostly working-class neighborhoods. Huge tracts of land in the Fillmore, Western Addition, and other neighborhoods were razed, and new buildings and districts were erected, including Japantown and the product district in Telegraph Hill, which moved to Alemany Boulevard. Many blacks were forced to move to housing projects in Hunters Point and across the Bay in Oakland. This massive urban renewal project also led to the building of Yerba Buena Gardens, the unpopular Embarcadero Freeway, and Embarcadero Center.

Arthur Ganz of the Argonaut Flag Corporation is shown in the 1950s with a seamstress sewing flags at Argonaut's new plant at 147 10th Street. Argonaut had a flag-manufacturing plant that was the most modern in the country, selling its products mostly to schools, steamship companies, and state and local governments in the West.

Children are pictured here on May 9, 1954, riding in imported sports cars during Guardsmen's Week in Golden Gate Park. For a small contribution to the Guardsmen Fund, boys and girls from the area had the thrill of riding in a sports car. The fund raised enough money to send 5,000 needy boys and girls to summer camp that year. With more than 1,000 acres open to the public, making it 20 percent larger than New York's Central Park, Golden Gate Park is treasured by San Franciscans. Thirteen million people visit the park annually, making it the third most popular park in the country. Looking at Golden Gate Park's lush vegetation and waterfalls, few would believe that until the 1870s, the land was entirely sand dunes. Field engineer William Hammond Hall prepared a topographic map and plan for the park site in 1870, and Hall and his assistant John McLaren refined the plan and stabilized the sand dunes by planting trees.

Sports cars roar away from the starting point of the Mayor's Trophy Race at Golden Gate Park in 1953. A crowd as big as 115,000 watched the annual event. Dion Holm, City Attorney, was the starter, and Hollywood's Ken Miller, driving an MG Special, won the race.

A group of San Franciscans enjoy folk dancing in Golden Gate Park on the afternoon of June 2, 1953.

Tourists visit the Japanese Tea Garden in Golden Gate Park on April 2, 1954. Built originally as the Japanese Village for the California Midwinter International Exposition of 1894, the Japanese Tea Garden was converted to a permanent exhibit at the suggestion of Japanese immigrant and gardener Mokato Hagiwara. Hagiwara and later his family became the garden caretakers until 1942, when they were forced to evacuate to an internment camp as a result of Executive Order 9066. During the war years, the garden was renamed the Oriental Tea Garden but became known as the Japanese Tea Garden in 1952. Today, the tranquil Japanese Tea Garden remains a popular destination for looking at the flowering cherry trees and other Japanese plants, beautiful birds, exotic koi swimming in the ponds, and Asian sculptures. Visitors to the garden's tea house can stop to sip a cup of green tea and sample delicious Japanese confections.

Machinists balance a 20-ton propeller in a shipyard on June 25, 1953, in Hunters Point. Built around 1870 and named after a wealthy landowner, Hunters Point was the site of a commercial shipyard and the West Coast's first drydocks. During both world wars, the U.S. Navy used the drydocks as a shipyard and naval base. Between World War II and 1974, the 500-acre shipyard employed 17,000 people at its peak. The Hunters Point area also became residential, with nearly 100 percent of the occupants being African-Americans who came from the South in the Second Great Migration during World War II to work in the Bay Area's naval shipyards. After the naval base closed in the postwar years, Hunters Point went into massive economic decline but has been in the process of gentrification since the late 1990s.

Pulitzer Prize-winning San Francisco columnist Herb Caen (April 3, 1916–February 1, 1997) is pictured here on October 28, 1953, talking on the phone at his desk. Affectionately nicknamed "Mr. San Francisco" for his deep knowledge and passion for his adopted city, Caen wrote a column for the *San Francisco Chronicle* from the late 1930s until his death in 1997, except for an eight-year stint in the 1950s next door at the *Examiner*. Caen was known for his series of essays titled *Baghdad-by-the-Bay* and his 1953 book, *Don't Call It Frisco*. He is credited with coining the word *Beatnik* in an April 2, 1958, column on the new cultural phenomenon happening in San Francisco's North Beach, as well as popularizing the term *hippie* during the Summer of Love in the Haight-Ashbury neighborhood in 1967. When Caen died in 1997, his funeral was one of the most well-attended events in San Francisco history.

People gather in Union Square on Christmas Eve 1953 to listen to the Golden Gate Park Band. "Merry Christmas to all, especially the pigeons" is inscribed on the original photo. Thousands of pigeons that fly around Union Square are known as San Francisco's "flying rats." Officials in San Francisco regularly look for ways to control the pigeon birthrate.

Marilyn Monroe, the iconic blond bombshell, and Joe DiMaggio, the New York Yankees baseball legend who grew up in San Francisco, are shown at San Francisco City Hall immediately after getting married on January 1, 1954. Monroe filed for divorce 274 days later, but, after her untimely death in 1962, DiMaggio arranged her funeral and had roses delivered to her crypt three times a week for the following two decades.

Pedestrians on the Golden Gate Bridge watch the Pacific Fleet enter San Francisco Bay on February 20, 1954. Though still wintertime, this was a wonderful spring-like day, and people flocked to the city's beaches and Land's End. Chief engineer Joseph Strauss conceived of the majestic marvel of engineering, which spans 1.7 miles and connects San Francisco to Marin County. When this depression-era public-works project was completed in 1937, the Golden Gate Bridge became the largest suspension bridge in the world. Painted the bold shade of "international orange" to stand out in the fog, the famous bridge is the only road exiting San Francisco to the north. Every day 100,000 vehicles cross the Golden Gate Bridge, the most photographed bridge in the world.

On May 15, 1954, Lieutenant Noel Taylor and his sons, Stephen and Roger, look at an exhibit in the Presidio of a target plane, one of the Sixth Army's many displays on Armed Forces Day, when thousands of Bay Area residents visited military installations to see big ships, planes, and guns. A Spanish Imperial outpost from 1776 to 1821 and subsequently owned by Mexico until 1846, the Presidio became the most important Army headquarters on the Pacific Coast from 1846 until 1994. Throughout the Cold War, it became a center of Nike missile development. Between the Korean War and 1972, Nike anti-aircraft defenses were based all around the area. By the 1970s, newer defense technology replaced the obsolete missiles, and all of the Nike facilities in the Bay Area except one were dismantled. The Presidio has been part of the Golden Gate National Recreation Area since 1994.

Here on May 17, 1954, is Old No. 51, a famed cable car on the O'Farrell, Jones & Hyde line, about to be retired from service. A crowd of people protested the replacement of O'Farrell, Jones & Hyde cable cars with gas buses and said farewell forever. Old No. 51 was the last car on the run and did not give up without a struggle, getting into the cable car barn at California and Hyde with the biggest and loudest load of passengers she ever carried. San Francisco's very first cable car ran down Clay Street on August 2, 1873. The California Street cable car continued to operate independently until 1952, when it became part of Muni. Six of the retired cable cars from the O'Farrell, Jones & Hyde line were taken on by the California Street line, including Old No. 51, which climbs up and down Nob Hill to this day. In 1964, the cable car system was designated a National Historic Landmark.

A decorated cable car is pictured here at the Cable Car Festival on April 23, 1955. The car commemorates the "Gay 90s" in San Francisco, referring to the city's joyful 1890s, a rather ironic description considering that San Francisco would become a mecca for homosexuals a few decades after this photo was taken.

This nighttime view of San Francisco looking eastward towards the Bay Bridge highlights the city's skyline in 1955. Missing at the time from the San Francisco skyline were the Bank of America building on California Street, the Transamerica Pyramid, the Embarcadero Center buildings, and many other downtown and financial district high-rises that were not built until the 1970s.

A Chinese drum corps marches in a parade in San Francisco in 1955. This group and similar marching bands and drum teams marched in San Francisco's annual Chinese New Year's Parade and other parades in the Bay Area and across the state.

On March 16, 1955, several hundred University of San Francisco students send off the school's basketball team at San Francisco International Airport as they board a TWA plane for Kansas City to play Colorado in the Final Four of the NCAA tournament. The Dons won 62-50 and went on to win the national championship. The Dons would win the national championship once again in 1956, with both the 1955 and 1956 teams powered by future Hall of Fame center Bill Russell. They have not celebrated a national title since.

St. Ignatius Church, pictured here on July 15, 1955, is actually the fifth church of that name to be built in San Francisco. Completed in 1914, the current church is built in Italian Renaissance and Baroque style and is located on the campus of the University of San Francisco. The church's hilltop location and its two spires and dome make St. Ignatius Church a prominent San Francisco landmark.

Worshipers enter Old St. Mary's Church on California and Grant streets for Good Friday services on March 31, 1956. Built in 1853 and 1854 from imported Chinese granite and New England bricks—scarce materials in Gold Rush San Francisco—Old St. Mary's was San Francisco's biggest building for a time. Brothels and other "un-Christian" activities surrounded the church into the twentieth century. Church leaders had hoped that the biblical quote, "Son, Observe the Time and Fly from Evil," prominently displayed on the front of the church clock, would resonate with neighborhood sinners, especially the prostitutes in the brothel located directly across the street, at eye level with the clock tower.

On June 13, 1957, Sister Eileen Catherine coaches (and here, umpires) boys in baseball at St. Cecilia School, a coeducational Catholic elementary school founded in 1930 during the Depression and located at 660 Vicente Street. Father John Harnett, the second pastor of St. Cecilia, built the grammar school for $80,000, and the Sisters of the Holy Names of Jesus and Mary were invited to staff the new school when it opened.

Students gather in the assembly room of Katherine Delmar Burke School in the fifties. Originally Miss Burke's School, it was opened in 1908 by Katherine Delmar Burke as an independent all-girls school. It moved to its Sea Cliff site at 195 32nd Avenue at California Street in the 1930s, where the campus remains today. The school used to go from kindergarten through high school, but in 1975 the high school, located in Pacific Heights, was discontinued, and the building was sold to the newly created San Francisco University High School. This fireplace was designed in the assembly room to make the girls feel more at home. Today, Burke's is one of three all-girls schools in the city and among the top-rated private schools in the Bay Area.

San Francisco mayor George Christopher, Town School for Boys headmaster Dr. Edwin Rich, Reverend Edward A. Wicher, and Pat McBaine, the 12-year-old student body president of Town School, are pictured during the dedication ceremony of the new Town School building on September 28, 1956, at its current location on Jackson Street in Pacific Heights. Town was founded in 1939 by the parents of students from Damon School, a private school that had closed. At the time this photo was taken, the school was the only all-boys elementary school in the city and had an enrollment of 300 students. Today, Town School is one of the top private schools in the Bay Area.

Vice-president Richard Nixon shakes hands with the dragon in the Double-Ten Parade in Chinatown on October 10, 1956. The parade celebrates the anniversary of the Chinese Republicans taking control of China from Emperor Ching in 1911. Double-Ten Day is celebrated in China, Taiwan, and Hong Kong and in overseas Chinese communities around the world. Nixon's visit to San Francisco occurred a few months after the August 1956 Republican National Convention was held in San Francisco, when President Dwight D. Eisenhower and Vice-president Nixon were renominated as the party's candidates for the 1956 presidential election. During the campaign, Nixon and his wife made many appearances around the country before being reelected in November.

On September 19, 1957, the U.S. Navy exploded a dummy atomic bomb on Treasure Island shot from Yerba Buena Island. Treasure Island was created for the Golden Gate International Exposition in 1939 from landfill dredged from San Francisco Bay. Named after the novel *Treasure Island* by Robert Louis Stevenson, who lived in San Francisco from 1879 to 1880, the island was supposed to be turned into a airport after the Exposition, but Mills Field on the San Francisco Peninsula was used instead. During World War II, Treasure Island became part of the Treasure Island Naval Base. Decommissioned in 1996, the island is now part of San Francisco but is still owned by the Navy. While the island is currently used for rental housing and occasional television filming, debates are continually waged about its long-term purpose.

Swimmers from the Dolphin Club race in San Francisco Bay on October 2, 1957. In 1877, John Wieland and his brothers, along with the Kehrlein brothers, all immigrants from Germany, founded the male-only Dolphin Club in San Francisco for swimming and rowing. Membership was limited originally to 25 men. It was not until 1976 that women were allowed to join the Dolphin Club. From 1957, when this photograph was taken, to this day, club members swim year-round in the waters of Aquatic Park, where temperatures vary from about 50 degrees Fahrenheit in January to about 61 degrees Fahrenheit in September.

Alcatraz is seen from the top of Hyde Street Hill on October 4, 1957. Spanish explorer Juan Miguel de Ayala, the first European to discover the island, referred to it in the 1770s as La Isla de los Alcatraces, meaning Pelican Island. In the 1850s, the Coast Guard was contracted to build the West's first lighthouse on the island. Alcatraz Island became an official military prison on August 27, 1861, and was used during the Civil War to imprison those whose loyalty to the Union was dubious, foreshadowing the island's future as a prison.

On October 12, 1957, a new 12-foot bronze statue of Christopher Columbus, designed by sculptor Vittorio di Colbertaldo, is dedicated at the top of Telegraph Hill in front of Coit Tower. The statue, which depicts Columbus gazing west towards the Golden Gate, was funded by Italy and the city of San Francisco. Coit Tower was built in 1933 at the bequest of Lillian Hitchcock Coit for beautification of the city of San Francisco.

During the 1950s, San Francisco's middle class was growing, and people had more disposable income than they had had in decades. Advertisements suggested that buying certain products or clothes would result in happiness. Showing pictures of the ideal home and the perfect, well-dressed family surrounded by all of the modern conveniences encouraged people to shop more, and the busiest time for shopping was the month before Christmas. In this photograph, taken on Friday, November 29, 1957, a crowd of San Franciscans cross the street at the intersection of Geary and Stockton streets at Union Square, a favorite place to shop in downtown San Francisco at the beginning of the holiday shopping season.

The Broadway Tunnel, seen in this fifties photograph that was taken looking west on Broadway from Grant Street, was opened in 1952. The tunnel passes underneath Russian Hill and provides a quick route for cars traveling between Chinatown and North Beach in the east and Russian Hill and Van Ness Avenue in the west. Seen on the right of Broadway before the entrance to the tunnel are Loui-Jo's Bar-B-Que and the San Carlos Club.

The cast of the floor show at Finocchio's Nightclub is pictured in a fashion parade on June 28, 1958. Joe Finocchio opened this club on June 15, 1936, with male cross-dressers performing as female impersonators in wigs and glitzy costumes. Finocchio's was a popular tourist destination until Joe Finocchio's widow closed the club on November 27, 1999. When poet Lawrence Ferlinghetti heard that Finocchio's had closed, he commented, "What a drag."

Lawrence Ferlinghetti is shown here on August 6, 1957, at his City Lights Bookstore, the hub of Beatnik activity and publishing in the fifties. The city of San Francisco was preparing for the case filed against Ferlinghetti for selling a book of poems, *Howl*, by Allen Ginsburg. The District Attorney's office prosecuted him for violating the Penal Code, which prohibits writing, composing, printing, publishing, or selling "any obscene pictures or print." The U.S. Customs Office in San Francisco had earlier confiscated copies of the book but was overruled by its Washington office, which did not view the book as obscene. J.W. Ehrlich, the high-priced trial lawyer, represented Ferlinghetti.

Over 100,000 baseball fans welcome San Francisco's new baseball team, the San Francisco Giants, in a parade on April 13, 1958, that ran along Montgomery Street to Market Street. A citywide obsession with the new team followed, and all-stars like Willie Mays and Willie McCovey became the new heroes of the day. The fact that the team came from New York gave a new air of prestige to the city. In the Giants' first game, the first major-league game to be played on the West Coast, the team beat the Dodgers 8-0 and won 83 games in their first year alone. In this picture taken from the seventh floor of the Sheraton Palace Hotel, San Francisco mayor George Christopher stands under the welcome sign. Reportedly, as he stood there, the crowd cheered that "George brought the Giants." For over 50 years, fans have eagerly anticipated another Giants parade down Market Street to celebrate a World Series win, but this has yet to occur. The team has made only three appearances in the World Series, losing in 1962, 1989, and 2002.

The aircraft carrier *USS Ticonderoga* is shown passing underneath the Golden Gate Bridge on April 25, 1958. The "Big T," as it was referred to, was at the end of a seven-month tour of the Western Pacific and was carrying 2,400 sailors at the time. The *Ticonderoga* was one of 24 *Essex*-class aircraft carriers built in America during World War II. Named after the famous fort of the American Revolution, it served in the Pacific during the second world war, earning five battle stars, and was decommissioned before its end. After updates, *Ticonderoga* was recommissioned in the early 1950s as an attack carrier and antisubmarine carrier. It was decommissioned one last time in 1973 and finally sold for scrap metal in 1975.

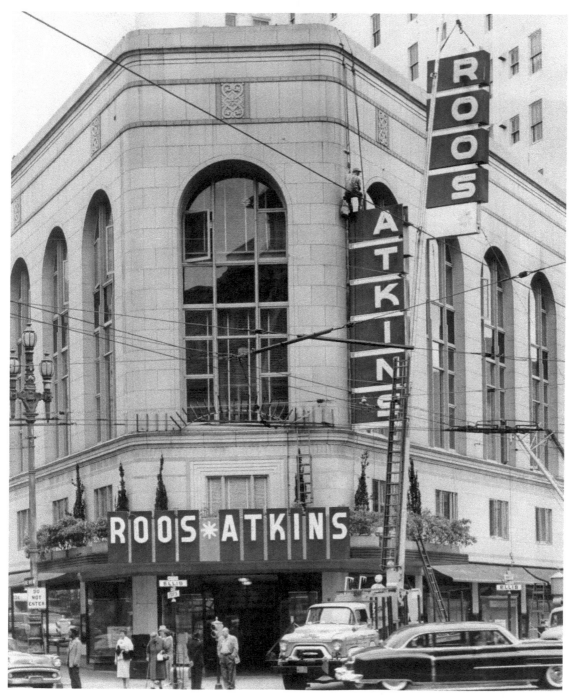

The upscale Roos-Atkins men's-clothing store is pictured at the intersection of Market, Stockton, and Ellis on July 28, 1958, marking the merger of the two firms that were started by Robert Atkins and the Roos brothers. Roos-Atkins operated stores throughout Northern California but closed all of them in the early 1990s following sagging sales.

The Emporium spreads holiday cheer to thousands of children on November 8, 1958. Santa Claus always came to the Market Street department store atop a cable car.

Judy Rae Wilson, Miss San Francisco 1958, is delivered to San Francisco Airport by a motorized California Street cable car on Saturday, September 13, 1958. She then flew via Western Airlines to Mexico City, where she took part in Independence Day festivities of the Mexican Republic on September 15.

On Friday, November 28, 1958, the intersection of Market and 5th streets is mobbed by well-dressed holiday shoppers looking to beat the crowds and start their holiday shopping at the wide range of downtown stores.

Ocean Beach has virtually disappeared under a layer of foamy surf during the extremely high tide, pictured here on January 8, 1959. High waves, a severe undertow, and the extremely cold Pacific waters make Ocean Beach treacherous for most swimmers, especially during high tide, though serious surfers can be found year-round in these waters.

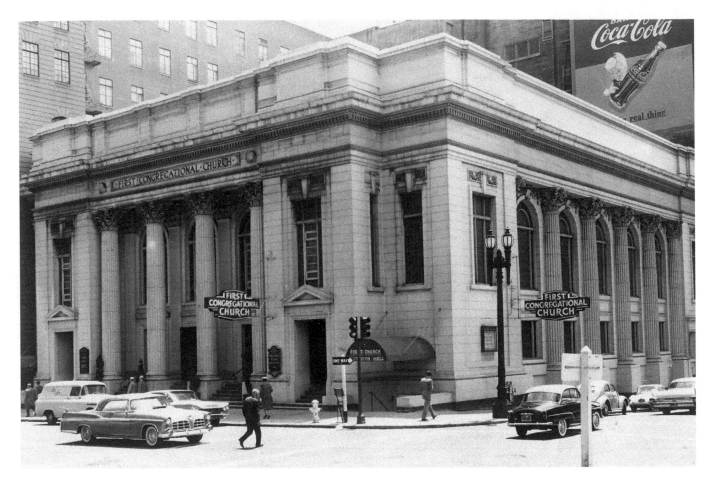

The First Congregational Church, located at 491 Post Street when this photo was taken on January 8, 1959, was celebrating its 110th birthday. The church opened in 1850 at Jackson Street and Virginia Place and had a membership of eight worshipers. It moved in 1853 to a new building at California and Dupont streets, and after membership grew, a new Gothic-style building was dedicated May 19, 1872. At the time of the 1906 Earthquake, the First Congregational Church had the largest Protestant-church membership in San Francisco. The Gothic steeple, a symbol of the 1872 building, crumbled in the earthquake, and a new building was dedicated in 1915. After a special service creating the United Nations was held here in 1946, flags from around the world were mounted in the sanctuary. The church moved again in 2001 and is now located at Polk and Bush streets.

The 1960s:

Protests, Hippies, and Civil Rights

Pictured here on June 13, 1962, the funeral procession for local politician and community advocate Albert Chow moves through the streets of Chinatown. Similar to many Chinese funeral processions, this one resembles a parade, led by police motorcycle escorts and a full-size marching band playing hymns. Carrying a large picture of Chow, family members and friends follow the band and throw out spirit money to ward off malicious ghosts. The parade stops at Chow's former homes, workplaces, and other places familiar to him so that his spirit can make one last visit.

Tourists look at Alcatraz Island on May 20, 1960, through telescopes located at Fisherman's Wharf. At the time, Alcatraz was still being used as a maximum-security federal prison.

Columbus Tower, shown here on April 3, 1960, was completed in 1907 following extensive damage to the construction site during the 1906 Earthquake. Its distinctive copper-green edifice is one of the few remaining San Francisco buildings designed in the flatiron style of early-twentieth-century American architecture. Also known as the Sentinel Building or the San Francisco Flatiron Building, the tower is now a designated landmark. The building once housed Caesar's, credited with creating the popular Caesar salad (other stories suggest Tijuana, Chicago, or other locales as the origin of the piquant dish). By the early 1970s, the building had fallen into a state of disrepair, and film director Francis Ford Coppola purchased and renovated it.

Pictured on September 12, 1960, a Balloon Derby at Stonestown commemorates the 50th anniversary of Frank Werner Co. shoe stores. The person whose balloon made the longest flight won a trip to Disneyland (which had just opened five years before) in a promotion sponsored by the popular shoe store.

President Dwight D. Eisenhower speaks at the Sheraton Palace Hotel on October 21, 1960. During his address to 1,800 people, the president criticized John F. Kennedy, the Democratic presidential nominee, when he denounced anyone who said that the United States had become a secondary power. Eisenhower's presidency brought prosperity to Americans and allowed many to achieve what they thought of as the "American dream." Although Eisenhower was a Republican and disliked government spending, he kept many of Franklin Roosevelt's New Deal Programs, expanded Social Security, increased minimum wage for workers, and even created the Department of Health, Education, and Welfare.

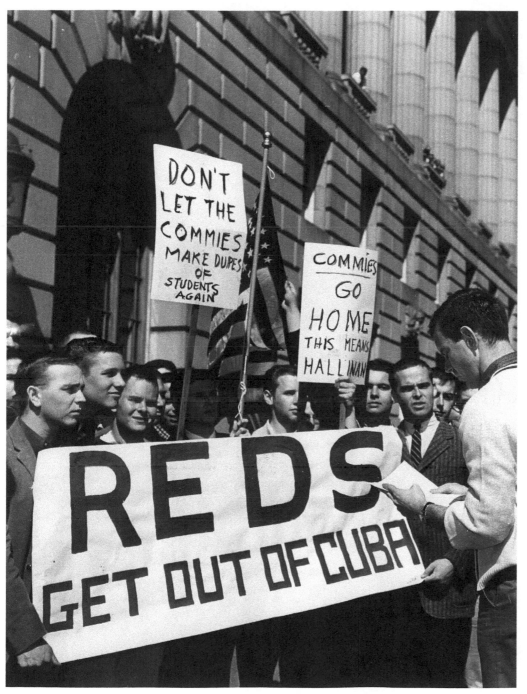

An anti-Castro group of young people is shown before the Federal Building clashing with pro-Castro supporters on April 20, 1961. The "pros" were from some Bay Area colleges, and the "antis" were from San Francisco State and the University of San Francisco. Fidel Castro was a leader of the 26th of July Movement in the Cuban Revolution, culminating when the American-backed Fulgencio Batista dictatorship was overthrown on New Year's Day, 1959. The Cuban Revolution was Marxist in nature, and Castro became closely allied with the Soviet Union during the Cold War. Once Castro took control, everything went under government control. It is estimated that at any given point, 20,000 dissenters were being tortured or imprisoned. Castro also put Cuban homosexuals in internment camps and had thousands of his own people executed. Hundreds of thousands of Cubans escaped to the United States by the early 1960s.

On July 24, 1961, Reverend Dr. Martin Luther King Jr. spoke at a huge Freedom Riders rally at the Cow Palace. Dr. King made an impassioned plea for stepped-up resistance to segregation to almost 15,000 people, a thousand of whom were whites. Ultimately, he raised $16,000 for the Freedom Riders. The civil-rights movement began in the 1950s and reached its height in the 1960s, adopting new tactics to achieve its aims modeled after the nonviolent, passive-resistant methods of Gandhi in India. Jim Crow laws were in effect in the South, and much of the country was still segregated. A major milestone was achieved on May 17, 1954, when the United States Supreme Court, in the landmark *Brown v. Board of Education* decision, declared the segregation of schools unconstitutional. Southern states were slow to comply with this ruling, and the National Guard had to be called out in many states to enforce it. King would be assassinated in the spring of 1968.

An aerial view of Golden Gate Bridge, recorded on August 9, 1961, shows the fog rolling in. San Francisco is surrounded on three sides by the frigid waters of the Pacific Ocean and San Francisco Bay, which combine with the heat from the California mainland to produce the thick fog that San Francisco is famous for. Because of this topography, there is little variation in average temperature between the seasons, and San Francisco maintains a yearly average close to 60 degrees Fahrenheit.

Danny Town and Patti Keate play on the sand dunes and ice plants during an open house at Fort Funston on October 30, 1961. The former military installation was built in 1938 and deactivated in 1948. The open house was sponsored by the Citizens Committee for Proposition B, the November 7 election bond issue, which would allow the city to buy 116 acres for $1.1 million, half the parcel's appraised value.

A group overlooks Seal Rocks from the Cliff House on Valentine's Day, 1963.

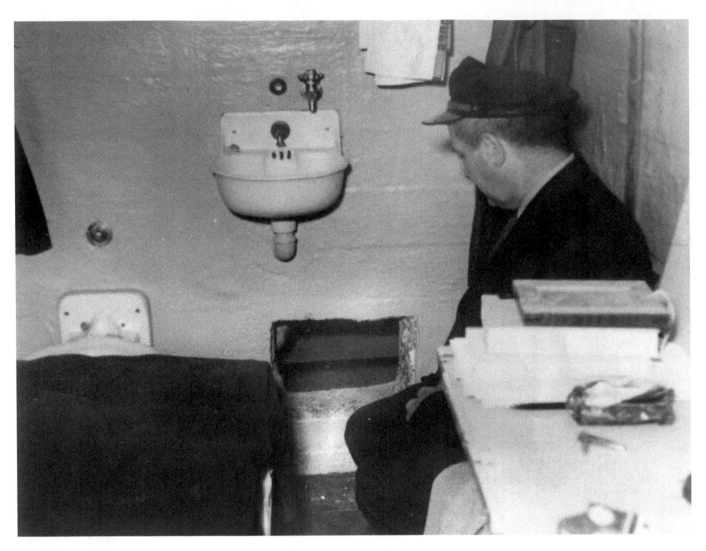

Believed to be an inescapable locale in the middle of San Francisco Bay, Alcatraz Island became a famous U.S. Federal Prison in 1934. From then on, many simply referred to the island and the prison itself as "the Rock." Frequently depicted in film and literature, it housed such notorious criminals as Al Capone and Robert Shroud, the "Birdman" of Alcatraz. There have been 14 separate escape attempts in its history as a federal prison, the most famous of which was carried out in June of 1962. Three inmates, Frank Lee Morris and brothers Clarence and John W. Anglin, dug a hole through their cell walls, climbed up a chimney to the ventilation shaft, which led to the roof, and climbed down to paddle away from the island on a rubber raft made from prisoners' raincoats. Pictured here on June 13, 1962, Senior Officer Waldron inspects a hole in the wall of escaped convict Frank Morris's prison cell. Spoonful by spoonful, Morris created the hole in the cell block.

The rush-hour commute on the Golden Gate Bridge is shown on August 24, 1962. At this time, city planners implemented a new plan to provide an extra lane to the direction with the most rush-hour traffic. Dividers were shifted, making four southbound lanes and only two northbound lanes during the morning rush from Marin County into San Francisco. The system continues to this day, with the opposing directions of traffic separated only by flimsy posts, though proposals for a more substantial but still movable wall-type barrier occasionally surface.

Women measure for points during a game on the bowling green in Golden Gate Park on September 10, 1962. Fifty years before, the first women's bowling green in America opened here in September of 1912 by Mayor James Rolph Jr. The club numbered 68 women when this was taken, and matches were held twice a week.

On President's Day, 1963, Laura Hortencia Palmarez sits on the statue of President Abraham Lincoln on Polk Street by City Hall. The statue outside City Hall was designed in bronze in 1928 by Armenian-American sculptor Haig Patigian, who also unveiled a statue of Thomas Starr King in 1831 in Washington, D.C. San Francisco was the site of an earlier statue of Abraham Lincoln as well. Artist Pietro Mezzara created a plaster statue of Lincoln in 1866, said to be the first statue of the 16th President in the western United States, but the statue was destroyed in the 1906 Earthquake.

Before the famous Fox Theatre, known as the "Showplace of the West," closed its doors in the winter of 1963, the management scheduled four farewell events for the public, each one packed to the theater's 4,651-person capacity. On Saturday, February 9, the second night of farewells, organist George Wright played his final number, "I Left My Heart in San Francisco," on the famous Wurlitzer theater pipe organ before it descended into the orchestra pit for the last time. The last Farewell to the Fox Benefit is pictured on February 16, 1963, shortly before the Fox lowered its curtains for the last time and closed its brass doors forever.

Lowell High School students, in tune with the spirit of student protest in San Francisco and around the country in the sixties, are pictured boycotting the school cafeteria on April 27, 1963. Strikers were angry because profits from the cafeteria's soft-drink machine were going to the citywide cafeteria fund and not into the school's student-body treasury. Student strikers wanted more money for better football equipment, improved dances, and aid for a former student in the Peace Corps in Africa. Even though this was the second strike, principal J.A. Perino did not expel anyone, explaining that the strikes were an indication of "springtime exuberance." Lowell, founded in 1856, is located near Lake Merced and is the oldest public high school west of the Mississippi in the continental United States.

San Francisco supervisor Clarissa McMahon addresses a crowd at the Civic Center Plaza on May 27, 1963. Twelve thousand marched up Market Street, singing the "Battle Hymn of the Republic" in protest against racial oppression. The event, organized by the San Francisco Church Labor Conference as an observance of Human Rights Day, was peaceful without any disturbances that were commonplace in strikes at this time.

Steve Matthews sits in a field of floats used to support harbor defense nets at Hunters Point Naval Shipyard on December 18, 1963.

In order to improve San Francisco–bound traffic, men with jackhammers chip away at 60-year-old Battery Lancaster foundations on February 7, 1964, to widen the approach at the Golden Gate Bridge southern end. Today, Battery Lancaster is adjacent to the bridge's toll plaza. Its emplacements are partially incorporated into the pedestrian walkway to the bridge and the Visitor Gift Center. The left side of the battery, which contains interior magazines, is visible today, and the gun platform has been filled with dirt and gravel.

Because the old Academy of Art campus at 431 Sutter Street was too small, the college moved in 1964 to a new building at 604 Sutter Street. The exodus was accomplished in just a single day, as 30 students carried all the equipment and supplies. Larry Herrera is pictured pulling model Alice Marie Beckman in a cart on moving day on April 30, 1964. Reportedly the largest art and design school in the United States, the Academy of Art University, founded in 1929, has nearly 16,000 students enrolled and occupies 31 buildings in downtown San Francisco.

Enrico Banducci, pictured on May 7, 1964, was the famed impresario of North Beach, who ran the hungry i nightclub in the basement of the International Hotel at Kearny and Jackson streets. Banducci bought the club in 1948 from the previous owner, Eric "Big Daddy" Nord, for $800 (which he had to borrow). Banducci helped launch the careers of a teenage Barbara Streisand, who made her debut there in the early 1960s, as well as Bill Cosby, Woody Allen, Richard Pryor, and others. Featured comedians performed in front of a red-brick wall, now a staple in comedy clubs, and felt uncensored, free to poke fun at American culture and politics. The meaning of the *i* in the hungry i was a bit ambiguous. It stood for either "intellectual," or, according to Banducci, for the "id" in Freudian thought. Banducci had a reputation for being an eccentric, which made him fit right into the San Francisco cultural scene. He married five times and always wore his trademark beret. Although it is estimated that he made as much as $10 million over the years from the club and other ventures, he spent all his money, went bankrupt, sold the club, and even served time in prison at one point.

The famous City of Paris department store in Union Square is pictured on July 5, 1964. During the Gold Rush, the French Verdier brothers opened a store called La Ville de Paris ("the City of Paris") on a ship in San Francisco Bay to cater to the needs of Argonauts passing through the city. In 1896, the business moved into a beautiful Beaux-Arts building, designed by architects John Bakewell and Arthur J. Brown, at the corner of Geary and Stockton streets in Union Square. It was demolished in 1981 and replaced with the Nieman Marcus that is there today, but the glass dome and part of the original rotunda from the City of Paris was salvaged and is still in the building.

The Castro Theatre at 429 Castro Street is pictured on August 12, 1964. People now know the Castro District as San Francisco's and the nation's gay haven, but at this point, the neighborhood was still largely a conservative Irish-Catholic area. The Nasser brothers, pioneers in the early theater business in San Francisco, founded the theater in 1922. It was designed by famed architect and interior designer Timothy L. Pfluger, who later gained notoriety for building the Top of the Mark lounge at the Mark Hopkins Hotel, the Patent Leather Bar at the St. Francis Hotel, and the Fairmont's Cirque and for overseeing design of the Bay Bridge and the Golden Gate International Exposition in 1939. The Castro, which seats 1,400, features a Spanish Colonial Baroque exterior and ornate Italian, Spanish, Asian, and even Art Deco interior.

A model poses at the Palace of Fine Arts lagoon in the Marina District on September 11, 1964. After the devastation of the 1906 Earthquake and fires, San Francisco began a massive rebuilding project, adding almost 20,000 new buildings to its streets within a few years. After nearly a decade of rebuilding, the city celebrated the 1915 Panama Pacific Exposition. Officially, it signified the completion of the Panama Canal, which substantially shortened the voyage to San Francisco from the East, but more than anything, this exposition was a tribute to the old city lost in the quake and a celebration of the rebuilt city's endurance. Architect Bernard Maybeck designed the Palace of Fine Arts for the exposition to resemble the grand structures of antiquity. Construction on the Palace began on December 8, 1913, and today, the Exploratorium science museum is housed in the Old Exhibition Hall.

The St. Mary's Chinese Girls Drum Corps march in the Columbus Day Parade on October 10, 1964. Their uniforms were carefully selected to reflect their Chinese heritage. This renowned group has marched at parades around the state and across the country for 60 years and has won over 300 first-prize awards and received other recognitions.

An aerial view of Candlestick Park shows 44,115 fans jammed into the park for the All-Star Game. Fans filled every seat, including ones installed temporarily for the game. In the bottom of the tenth inning, the National League came back on an "All-Star" rally: Hank Aaron singled, Willie Mays doubled, and Roberto Clemente singled and brought home both game-winning runs. When first constructed, Candlestick Park had an open design in the outfield, which made it highly susceptible to cold high-speed winds from the Bay. The outfield area was enclosed with the expansion of the upper deck in 1971 to expand seating capacity for the San Francisco 49ers, though the view of the Bay was lost and the winds became more unpredictably swirling and just as cold.

San Francisco Giants baseball heroes Felipe Alou, Jim Davenport, Willie Mays, Juan Marichal, and Orlando Cepeda, from left to right, are shown en route to the 1962 All-Star game.

High-school students sand down wooden seats at Candlestick Park on July 21, 1964, during the SOS (Save our Stockings) project to protect ladies' stockings from snagging and tearing on the wood. This project was part of the "work creation" program sponsored by the Recreation-Park Department, which sent 32 teens into action against Candlestick Park's wooden seats. This five-day sanding operation provided summertime jobs to high-school students.

The Olympic Club "Polar Bears" run out of the frigid Pacific Ocean in 1965 after their annual New Year's Day dip. The Olympic Club is America's oldest athletic club, founded in 1860, with an active membership of over 5,000.

Old and new San Francisco are juxtaposed as modern skyscrapers serve as the backdrop for these beautiful turn-of-the-century Victorians on Steiner Street, pictured on February 27, 1965. This row of houses, located in Alamo Square near the Western Addition, are the most famous "Painted Ladies" in San Francisco. This stretch, also known as "Postcard Row" because of how prominently they figure in images of San Francisco, was built between 1892 and 1896 by developer Matthew Kavanaugh, who lived next door at 722 Steiner. The family in the 1980s sitcom *Full House* lived in one of the Painted Ladies, which was shown at the beginning of each episode while the opening theme song played.

The Vietnam War was probably the least popular war in modern history. Protests in American cities and rural areas became commonplace in the mid-1960s and into the 1970s. Many citizens were opposed to the brutality and seeming senselessness of the war. In 1964, President Lyndon B. Johnson announced an escalation of the American involvement in Vietnam, and students at the University of California at Berkley and at dozens of campuses across the country expressed strong opposition to the war through demonstrations and protests. In April 1965, a major antiwar march took place in Washington, D. C. In this photograph, taken in San Francisco on April 17, 1965, a group of women push strollers down Oak street on the way to the Federal Building in San Francisco as they lead a protest against the Vietnam War.

Motorized cable cars, mounted on Ford C-600 chassis purchased from Hughson Ford, are pictured on May 8, 1965, after having been used for promotional purposes by airlines and department stores. Arnold Gridley, president of Cable Car Advertisers; Bob Hellman, vice-president and general manager of Hughson, and Jerry Urbach, truck manager of Hughson, stand in front of the cars.

Sandy Harrison and Corinne Greaves visit the historic sailing ship *Balclutha* at Fisherman's Wharf on May 19, 1965. The wooden beauty with whom the ladies are posing formed the prow of the old windjammer. The *Balclutha* set sail for San Francisco on January 15, 1887, arriving after 140 days at sea, and has stayed there ever since. Its complex rigging and 25 sails required a crew of 26 men. The three-mastered steel-hulled square-rigged ship was built to deliver cargo around the world. It traveled around Cape Horn at the tip of South America 17 times. In the late nineteenth century, it delivered a large cargo of alcohol to the city, which at that time was in high demand. Tourists can now visit the historic ship at the Hyde Street Pier.

· The front entrance of Sutro Baths Ice Skating Rink is pictured in March 1966. Adolph Sutro had earned a reputation as a populist, a man of the people who provided entertainment and cultural diversions for regular people at affordable rates. Despite the remote location of the Sutro Baths and Cliff House in the Outside Lands of the city, people came out in throngs. When other railroads wanted to price-gouge customers going out to Ocean Beach, Sutro simply built his own railroad, the Ferries & Cliff House Railroad, which went form Presideo Avenue and California through the sand dunes of the Outside Lands, along Land's End, to the Sutro Baths and Cliff House. At one point, the Baths reopened as "Tropic Beach," and they were converted to an ice-skating rink later. In 1952, he sold the baths for $250,000 to George Whitney, proprietor of nearby Playland at the Beach.

After the 1966 fire at Sutro Baths, developers wanted to convert the site into apartments and a shopping complex, but instead it became part of the Golden Gate National Recreation Area when the National Park Service bought it for $5 million in 1980. The ruins of the former Sutro Baths are pictured here long after the historic structure mysteriously burned down.

Students from
Sunnyside
Elementary School
pose with a Muni
railway operator
on December 14,
1966. This public
elementary school,
named after its
neighborhood,
is located at 250
Foerster Street, not
far from the Geneva
Yard and Car Barn,
Muni's primary site
for storing historic
streetcars.

On September 8, 1967, Mayor John F. Shelley accepts a statue of Juan Bautista de Anza (who led an expedition of colonists from Mexico to settle in present-day San Francisco) from Governor Luis Encinas of Sonora, Mexico. Serving from 1964 to 1968, Shelley was the first Democratic mayor elected in San Francisco in 50 years, starting an unbroken line of Democratic mayors in the city that continues to this day. His term spanned very troubled times in the city's and country's history, including many strikes over unfair hiring practices, the Bayview/Hunters Point riots of 1966, and the Summer of Love in 1967. After riots broke out in Bayview/Hunters Point on September 27, 1966, when a white officer shot and killed a black youth accused of stealing a car, the mayor called a citywide state of emergency. Shelley appointed the city's first African-American supervisor, Terry Francis.

A man is pictured in the Haight in 1967, the year of the Summer of Love, also called the Long, Hot Summer. On January 14, 1967, 30,000 people gathered for the first-ever Human Be-in in Golden Gate Park, the precursor to the Summer of Love. Street artist performed for free, and drugs were cheap and plentiful. That summer, over 100,000 people converged on the Haight, bringing the hippie counterculture movement into public awareness. It was a social experiment as much as anything else, as young people gathered around a shared culture of sexual freedom, mind-altering drugs, communal living, and political ideology.

People are pictured hanging out in the Haight. In the aftermath of the Summer of Love, the neighborhood fell back into decline in the seventies and eighties. With citywide gentrification in the 1990s and an influx of new young urban professionals and people in search of the hipster lifestyle, the Haight saw an upswing. Businesses there decided to capitalize on the neighborhood's hippie legacy, and the Haight was turned into a tourist attraction. Haight-Ashbury still evokes images of flower children, hippies, drugs, and counterculture, and it remains a center for independent business, restaurants, thrift stores, music, and bookstores.

Police attempt to control the riots at San Francisco State College, now San Francisco State University, in 1968. The student strikes made global headlines. Led by the Third World Liberation Front, the strikers had the goal of creating an ethnic-studies department, as well as protesting the Vietnam War. A series of protests there had been going on since 1966, including sit-ins, teach-ins, rallies, and marches—and violent confrontations with the police. The largest and longest-running strike lasted from the fall of 1968 until March 1969, when police representing multiple jurisdictions occupied the campus and arrested over 700 people. College president S. I. Hayakawa even pulled out the wires from speakers atop a van in the midst of a rally. By the following spring, the strike ended with the creation of the College of Ethnic Studies.

Mayor Joseph Alioto (February 12, 1916 – January 29, 1998; second to right) served as mayor of San Francisco from 1968 to 1976 during a time of major turmoil and change in San Francisco. He worked to reduce taxes and crime, was a major force behind the development of BART, the Transmaerica Building, and the Embarcadero Center and brought more minorities into city government. Alioto and others are pictured at a dedication of new Muni buses on June 24, 1969. The popular GMC "New Look" buses served as the backbone of Muni's diesel bus fleet until they were retired in the 1990s.

In the 1960s, Native Americans were the poorest American ethnic group, with unemployment rates ten times the national average and a life expectancy 20 years shorter than the national average due to poverty and disease. The civil-rights movement inspired young Native American activists to also fight for their rights. On November 20, 1969, Richard Oakes, along with over 100 Indians and groups of Indian students, took over Alcatraz and started a 19-month occupation of the island. The goal of this occupation was to raise awareness among the general American public to the plight of the destruction of the traditional Indian way of life, and the need to achieve self-determination among American Indian tribes. The Indian Occupation on Alcatraz is pictured here on November 20, 1969.

An aerial view of Alcatraz is pictured during the Indian Occupation, when several American Indians either lived on the island or helped provide food, water, and money for the occupation. The occupiers endured harsh conditions on "the Rock" for over a year and a half without adequate water, heat, or electricity. As the Alcatraz Occupation gained more international attention, thousands came to the city from across the country to show their support for the rise of "Red Power." On June 11, 1971, U.S. marshals, FBI agents, and GSA federal protective officers removed the remaining 15 Indians, consisting of six men, four women, and five children. The occupation brought a resurgence of pride for native cultures and traditions and temporary freedom from control of the federal government. It signified a major milestone of Indian activism during the 1960s and 1970s and set the stage for further demonstrations that followed in the Indian Activism Movement, including Wounded Knee II in 1973.

The 1970s:
Continued Protests, a Divided Country, and Conclusion of the Vietnam War

A floral display outside the Conservatory of Flowers was created for the Golden Gate Park Centennial in July 1970. The oldest wood and glass conservatory in North America, the Conservatory of Flowers opened to the public in 1879 and is a city, state, and national historic monument. James Lick, and early San Francisco pioneer who participated in the Gold Rush and was the wealthiest man in California at the time of his death, bought construction materials for the conservatory but died in 1876 before it was built. San Francisco bought the conservatory for the park as part of the city's beautification campaign to offer open spaces for the rising urban population. The beautiful Victorian botanical greenhouse is the oldest building in the park.

The Grand Theatre at 2665 Mission Street is pictured in 1970. By the early 1900s, Mission Street had a high concentration of movie theaters and stores and was dubbed the "Mission Miracle Mile." Historically, the Mission District has always been home to many immigrants, including the Jewish, Irish, and Germans in the nineteenth and early twentieth centuries. After the 1906 Earthquake and fires, many displaced people and businesses relocated to the Mission, and the street became a major thoroughfare. The Irish and the Italians remained in the area long after the earthquake, and later, Mexicans and then Beatniks settled there. Mission Miracle Mile is now the main working-class shopping street for the 60,000 living nearby, and at night, young people from all parts of the city flock to the area for its ethnic restaurants and trendy bars.

A collision of freighters beneath the Golden Gate Bridge cause a massive oil spill in 1971. Here, citizens at Ocean Beach clean up the spill. One of the legacies of the hippie movement was the rise of environmentalism. Earth Day, which originated with peace activist John McConnell in 1969, is celebrated annually at the Spring Equinox, around March 20. America's first Earth Day Proclamation, which promoted the cleanup of streets, parks, and beaches, was given by San Francisco mayor Joseph Alioto on March 21, 1970.

Ghirardelli Square at Beach and Larkin streets is a San Francisco landmark. Located near Fisherman's Wharf, the square features a variety of shops and restaurants, including the wildly popular Ghirardelli ice-cream shop. During the Gold Rush, Italian immigrant Domingo Ghirardelli came to California and sold confections to miners in the gold fields. In 1852, he founded his first chocolate factory in San Francisco at the corner of Broadway and Battery. In 1893, he bought the entire block of what would become Ghirardelli Square as the headquarters for his Ghirardelli Chocolate Company. In 1967, the production of the chocolate moved to San Leandro, but San Franciscans and tourists alike still go to Ghirardelli Square in search of the best ice-cream sundaes in town. Prisoners at Alcatraz were said to have salivated over the aroma of fresh chocolate wafting over the Bay.

The Transamerica Pyramid, San Francisco's most famous skyscraper, is shown in middle-stage construction in 1971. Construction began in 1969 and was completed in 1972, forever changing the San Francisco skyline. The landmark was built to house the Transamerica Corporation and is still the company's logo. Architect William Pereira designed the 850-foot tall, 48-floor building, and until 1974, it was the tallest skyscraper west of the Mississippi and remains one of the 200 tallest buildings worldwide. The Pyramid exterior is covered in crushed quartz, giving it the white color it is known for. In 1999, it became the headquarters of the Dutch insurance company AEGON. Although the observation deck closed after September 11, 2001, the 212-foot spire houses cameras that form a virtual observation deck, controlled and viewed by visitors in the lobby.

San Francisco's Twin Peaks are two high hills in the center of the city, the second highest points in the city after Mt. Davidson. The surrounding neighborhood is also called Twin Peaks. On a clear day, the views of the city and Bay from the top of the peaks are stunning, as is evident in this November 1972 picture.

The Transamerica Pyramid dominates the San Francisco skyline as seen in this March 3, 1973, photograph that was taken from the Mark Hopkins Hotel at the top of Nob Hill.

A favorite ride at Playland at the Beach was the Big Dipper roller coaster, designed by Arthur Looff and opened in 1922. At one point on the scary ride, which took one minute and seven seconds, the cars dropped over 80 feet. George Whitney purchased the Big Dipper in 1936, but the wooden roller coaster was torn down in 1955 when it failed to meet safety regulations. Although Playland began declining in popularity in the 1960s, the Big Dipper was replaced by a smaller steel roller coaster, the Alpine Racer, which met the new safety standards. The Alpine Racer had some scary hairpin turns on the flat top and made riders feel like the cars were going over the edge. However, many San Franciscans believed the Alpine Rider, shown here in 1971, was less exciting than the Big Dipper.

The Mad Mine ride at Playland at the Beach, described in nearby signs as a dark ride where monsters are welcome, is shown on its final day of service, September 4, 1972.

It was a sad scene on September 4, 1972, when the merry-go-round at Playland at the Beach closed forever, 58 years after it opened. In the postwar years, the amusement park's management closed down some of the most beloved attractions, such as the Big Dipper roller coaster and Chutes at the Beach, and the park was never the same. After Whitney's death in 1958, Playland's management was passed on to his son and then to Bob Frazier and was eventually sold to developer Jeremy Ets-Hokin in 1971. The famous carousel has been refurbished and is now located at the Yerba Buena Gardens.

After Playland at the Beach was torn down in 1972, the lost remained vacant for nearly a decade before expensive, nondescript condominiums eventually replaced the beloved park. The construction site of the would-be Ocean Beach apartments is pictured here in June 1973. The lot remained vacant for a decade afterwards as punishment from the city because the contractors did not have a demolition permit. As Playland was being demolished, local neighborhood children salvaged Playland memorabilia from the dumpsters and saved many historic and antique items from the park. They are now available for public viewing at a museum 20 miles away in El Cerrito, aptly called Playland-Not-At-The-Beach.

The flower-topped Hyde Street cable car heads down Russian Hill towards the San Francisco waterfront with its route reflected in the sideview mirror of a parked car. Nineteen of the city's cable cars were elaborately decorated for their Centennial Celebration in August 1973. Russian Hill is an upscale neighborhood known for its charming stores and restaurants as well as beautiful views of the city. It got its name after people discovered the graves of Russian fur traders atop the hill during the Gold Rush. To the north of Russian Hill is Fisherman's Wharf, to the south is Nob Hill, to the west are Pacific Heights and the Marina, and to the east is North Beach.

Dianne Feinstein shakes hands with a new student officer at Sir Francis Drake Elementary School in December 1973. Today, Feinstein is senior U.S. senator from California. She served as mayor of San Francisco from 1978, after Mayor George Moscone was assassinated, and was elected and reelected afterwards, serving until 1988. In a decade when women fought for equality in society, she blazed the trail for the women's movement as she set many milestones—becoming the first female president of the San Francisco Board of Supervisors in 1969 and San Francisco's first (and only to date) female mayor as well as the first woman to serve the U.S. Senate from California and the first woman who presided at a Presidential inauguration.

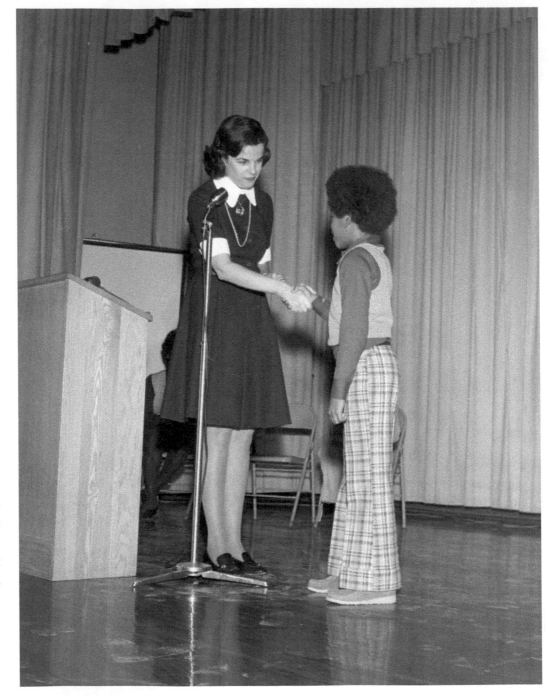

A taiko drummer plays in the Japanese Tea Garden at Golden Gate Park for the Cherry Blossom Festival in the spring of 1974. Today, the two-weekend festival is an annual celebration of Japanese culture. It features Japanese music, including taiko drums, dance, martial-arts demonstrations, tea ceremonies, fashion, and food. Seiichi Tanaka, a postwar immigrant who studied taiko in Japan, brought the styles and teachings to America when he formed the first American taiko group in 1968, called San Francisco Taiko Dojo.

This panorama of San Francisco is seen in October 1974 through the windows of Henri's Room at the Top, a restaurant on the 46th floor of the San Francisco Hilton Hotel. Henri's, which today is Cityscape Bar and Restaurant, used to feature birdcages and go-go girls. The Hilton first opened in 1971 and, following and expansion in 1987, is today the West Coast's largest hotel, with over 1,900 rooms.

This aerial view of downtown San Francisco in February 1975 is what motorists driving northbound from the San Francisco Peninsula on the 101 Freeway see just before the fork in the highway: traffic headed along 101 to the Civic Center and the Golden Gate Bridge veering to the left, and traffic headed for downtown and the Bay Bridge staying to the right on the 80 Freeway. Visible on the San Francisco skyline are (from left) the Hartford Building, the Bank of America World Headquarters, the Transamerica Pyramid, the Aetna and Wells Fargo buildings. Coit Tower on Telegraph Hill is seen at left.

The Telegraph Landing Condominiums are seen in this 1975 photograph, with Coit Tower visible in the background. It is hard to imagine the San Francisco skyline without Coit Tower. Heiress Lilly Hitchcock Coit left a third of her fortune to her beloved San Francisco, as she put it, "to be expended in an appropriate manner for the purpose of adding to the beauty of the city, which I have always loved." Architects Arthur Brown Jr. and Henry Howard designed the structure and denied the popular urban legend that it was built to look like a firehose to honor the firemen of the 1906 Earthquake.

The Peace Plaza at the Japantown Center is pictured in the seventies. San Francisco's Japantown, known as Nihonmachi in Japanese, is America's oldest Japantown. In 2006, Japantown celebrated its centennial anniversary in its present location in the Western Addition. Like the Chinese immigrants before them, the Japanese faced discrimination, immigration restrictions, segregation, and violence when they began arriving in the late 1800s and early 1900s. After the 1906 Earthquake, the Western Addition was one of the only Japanese enclaves in the city that was not destroyed. The Japanese government donated almost a quarter of a million dollars to the city to rebuild. The Peace Plaza, pictured here, was developed in the mid-1960s, and the Japantown center was completed in 1968. Today, Japantown houses most of the city's Japanese businesses.

The San Francisco Cherry Blossom Festival Parade takes place in Japantown each spring as a demonstration of Japanese cultural history and pride. In 2010, the Cherry Blossom Festival celebrated its 43rd year. When it began in April 1967, San Francisco was witnessing ongoing civil-rights and antiwar struggles and a revival of pride among ethnic groups. More than 150,000 people watch the annual festival, which celebrates Japanese culture and springtime in Japantown. San Francisco's Japantown is only one of three remaining Japantowns in the United States.

A tree-shaded street in Jackson Square, pictured in March 1975, is part of the old Barbary Coast of San Francisco. After the Gold Rush, it quickly gained a reputation as a seedy district known for its sinful pleasures, crime, saloons, prostitution, gambling halls, and opium dens. It was also an infamous spot for "shanghaiing," the slave-labor practice in which unwary victims were beaten or drugged and kidnapped to surrender for years of service on ships headed to far-off ports, such as Shanghai. The area was destroyed in the Great Earthquake and fires of 1906 and never quite reached its prequake reputation for debauchery. Many of the buildings were built of brick brought around Cape Horn, and some buildings still have "shanghai" holes in the cellar, where many an unwary Barbary Coaster began an unwanted sea voyage.

Harvey Milk, pictured in June 1977 in front of his store, Castro Camera, was a San Francisco County supervisor and the unofficial "Mayor of Castro Street." He was the first openly gay official of any big American city to be elected to office. Milk was born in Woodmere, N.Y., to a Jewish family on May 22, 1930. He served in the Korean War and was dishonorably discharged when his homosexuality was discovered, but he remained closeted for many years after that, working as an investment analyst on Wall Street. Milk moved to San Francisco's Castro Street in the late 1960s, at the time a neighborhood in transition from an Irish-Catholic to a gay neighborhood, and opened his camera store. After multiple tries, he was elected in 1977 to the Board of Supervisors.

Supervisor Harvey Milk sits in the Board of Supervisors Chambers in City Hall at the Budget Hearings in 1978. In 1978, he and Mayor George Moscone were shot to death in San Francisco's City Hall by Dan White, a supervisor who had resigned and then wanted his job back. White was convicted of the lesser crime of manslaughter and not murder because of the now infamous "Twinkie defense": his lawyers claimed that he was temporarily insane due to poor diet, too much junk food, and stress. When White got only a seven-year sentence, 40,000 San Franciscans came out to march in protest, and some rioted. He served only five years of his sentence before being released but ended up committing suicide after he returned to San Francisco. Milk once said that, "if an assassin's bullet should go through my head, then let it destroy every closet door." He inspired other homosexuals to run for office and many thousands of gays to come out of the closet.

The Balboa movie theater at 38th and Balboa in the Richmond District is pictured in 1978. Samuel H. Levin opened the Balboa on February 7, 1926, as a family-oriented theater. It remains one of the few independent theaters in San Francisco today.

This photograph provides a stunning aerial view of downtown San Francisco. The Transamerica Pyramid in the foreground and the four Embarcadero Center buildings dominate the picture. The Bay Bridge is visible in the upper left-hand corner.

Notes on the Photographs

These notes, listed by page number, attempt to include all aspects known of the photographs. Each of the photographs is identified by the page number, a title or description, photographer and collection, archive, and call or box number when applicable. Although every attempt was made to collect all data, in some cases complete data may have been unavailable due to the age and condition of some of the photographs and records.